BIG BROT

BOOKS

First published 2001 by Channel 4 Books
an imprint of Pan Macmillan Ltd
Pan Macmillan, 20 New Wharf Road, London, N1 9RR
Basingstoke and Oxford

Associated companies throughout the world

www.panmacmillan.com

ISBN 07522 6200 9

9 8 7 6 5 4 3 2 1

A CIP catalogue record for this book is available from the British Library.

Designed and typeset by seagulls

Printed and bound in Great Britain
by the Bath Press, Bath

This book accompanies the television series *Big Brother* made by Bazal for Channel 4.

Executive Producer: Ruth Wrigley
Series Executive Producer: Conrad Green

'EXPECT THE UNEXPECTED.'

GETTING TO KNOW YOU

'When I first came in, I considered myself a natural leader.'

PAUL

'Guess the colour of my mobile phone cover. It's pink snakeskin!'

HELEN

'You are a bit of a watcher, like me.'

STUART to Amma

‘I might act the fool, but I’m not a fool.’

BUBBLE

'I've never drunk cider..

'For my job I can sit and talk to strange men about anything and sound witty and charming and full of life. In here I sound as dull as ditchwater.'

AMMA

'I'd want them to get out of the suitcase, put themselves on me and walk me for that price.'

BUBBLE when Josh says his Gucci trousers cost £2,500

I've never eaten curry.'

BRIAN

'It's been the most terrifying experience of my life, being with you all and trying to adapt to that. You have seen the worst side of me, the most neurotic, the most manic, insecure side.'

PENNY before discovering she is to be evicted

'You are the funniest man I have ever met.'

BUBBLE to Brian, before he leaves the house

'That's fantastic, that is. Does he know?'

HELEN to Bubble, who is balancing three juggling balls on Brian's head

'Vanessa's a lucky woman. Dean is such a treasure.'

BRIAN's familiar description of Dean

'Sometimes I want to boil over and scream at someone but hey, they might think I'm a loony.'

JOSH in the Diary Room

'I must be a bit of a sicko. I get a kick out of mad circumstances, just like I get a kick out of being nominated.'

PAUL after his row with Amma, and surviving three votes for eviction

'I look like a transvestite killer Apache scout.'

DEAN when he is dressed as Narinder for the 'Dynasty'-style soap

'The thing you have over everyone else is that you are a genuinely caring person, and it's very visible. Hurray, Liz is capable of a bit of paranoia. We all do it.'

AMMA when Liz is worrying about being nominated

'When I was younger my head would have swelled. But I've matured a lot in the last few years.'

PAUL to Helen, after surviving the fourth eviction vote

'She's got a tan on the inside of her mouth.'

DEAN on Helen's constant chatter

'I thought I would go in the first week, because I'm too loud for some people. Then in the second week I thought I wouldn't go, because people would realize I wasn't a fucking idiot. Now they've seen the idiot, they've seen the other side of me, and they just think I'm a pain in the ass.'

BUBBLE

'I'm thinking about reading more books and taking country walks. I've been quite ignorant. I think they think I was raised as a child, blindfolded.'

BRIAN

'I feel such an ignoramus – I didn't know Roquefort was made from a sheep.'

LIZ after the cheese-tasting task

'I lied about mine.'

BUBBLE to Helen, who wants to know why she has fewer GCSEs than anyone else

'I do like girlie girls, but I do like an air of intelligence, otherwise it would do your head in.'

PAUL

'Oh my God. I'm so fat. I'm never going to have anyone to love me.'

BRIAN after discovering his waist size has increased by two inches

'I have lived my adult life like an international pop star.'

PAUL in the den with Helen

'They get on really well and have serious conversations with long words.'

HELEN on Dean and Liz

'I think I'll be like Bridget Jones.'

BRIAN

'If you hadn't come in, you wouldn't have met any of us, especially me.'

HELEN to Josh

'There would be a beach, palm trees, people would come there to re-learn what it is to be a human being. There would be music, dancing, no alcohol, there might be some nudity.'

LIZ on her Utopia

'I'd like to go to Ethiopia or somewhere like that. I can't build an orphanage but I could make the kids laugh and dress them and teach them something.'

BRIAN on what he wants to do before he dies

'A Mercedes convertible,
Gucci shoes, a Gucci handbag
and a trip to the Oscars.'

HELEN on what she wants to do before she dies

'You look at the girl and
you can't help but smile.'

BRIAN on Helen

'Tell you what, I'm used to talking
over hairdryers all the time.'

HELEN to Liz, on why she is so loud

'She said,

'If you've been lying and you're really straight...'

PAUL to Brian, when he helps Liz take her bikini top off

'How can I still look gay
when I'm dressed like this?'

BRIAN dressed as a cowboy, to Dean, who replies

'You just do. You look more gay.'

"Are you just trying to be fashionable?"

BRIAN on his mother's reaction when he told her he was gay

'Dad said, "You're not how I wanted you to turn out and your life's not perfect, but you're still my number one son and I love you."'

JOSH on telling his father he was gay

'We know what gay blokes do but not how you do it.'

HELEN as she and Narinder probe Josh for details

'It's alright for you Brian, you're gay. I'm straight. You haven't got friends like I've got… I'll never hear the end of this... I didn't think I was going to have to dress like a homosexual.'

DEAN on dressing in Helen's work uniform

‘Dove is a bird, isn’t it?’

HELEN

BITCHING

'Penny's cooked it.'

BUBBLE

'He doesn't know the name of the first man on the moon, for God's sake. To talk about Posh and Becks, Jennifer Lopez, Destiny's Child is climbing down. It's beneath me.'

DEAN on talking to Brian and Helen

'Pretend you're hitting her with a psychic-hitting stick.'

LIZ to Stuart, on coping with Penny

'She's harsh and scary.'

AMMA on Narinder

'It's constant. Lorinda, Serena, Serinda, Narina, Uranda – from everyone apart from Stuart, who's a sweetheart, and Dean. Have they never met an Asian person before?'

NARINDER on the housemates' inability to grasp her name

'She has to have a disagreement with everybody.'

NARINDER on Amma

'You could beat Penny senseless, mug her, take all her clothes and leave her at the side of the road and the next day say sorry and Penny would say, "That's OK, I love you."'

BRIAN on Penny

'I've never seen a man who looks in a mirror so many times...You are just a poser, naturally.'

AMMA to Paul

'Paul's probably a bright boy but his common sense is lacking. He only has one topic of conversation: girls and going out.'

AMMA

'I will kill you if you did that.'

NARINDER to Brian, after he jokes that he will become best friends with Amma if Narinder goes

'I was talking to them and I could feel the shutters coming down, the plug coming out of the socket.'

LIZ telling Dean about talking to Paul and Helen

'In all honesty, I was very bored here. You lot aren't the kind of people I would mix with. You did bore me.'

NARINDER's eviction speech

'Penny comes too much into my personal space. If she makes eye contact she takes it as an invitation for her touchy-feely ways.'

LIZ in the Diary Room

'He spits a lot

'Me and Penny are getting worse and worse and worse. If she pushes me too much, I'll flip.'

AMMA

'People must relate to him. But what people? With all due respect, they must be ten years old, like *Star Wars* and be able to kick their legs high.'

BRIAN on why Paul repeatedly survives the eviction votes

which I don't like.'

LIZ nominating Paul

'A lot of them are so irrational and melodramatic and so not real… Why do you have to fucking yell about everything? Why do you have to speak over everybody? Why do you never listen? Why can't you be normal? Why can't I smack you over the head? Why do you make me feel like this? Why am I going insane?'

LIZ rants to Dean about Helen

'She constantly gives me hacky looks.'

NARINDER on Helen

'I want to stay and bitch.'

NARINDER on why she does not want to be evicted

RUNNING THE HOUSE

'I'm the new porridge kid in town.'

BUBBLE after Penny left

'I've made a whole meal on my own.'

HELEN after making porridge

'I am the Porridge Princess now, aren't I?'

HELEN

'It tastes like finishing plaster.'

DEAN on Helen's porridge

'Is jelly cooked?'
HELEN

'I feel like God in here.'

PENNY taking charge of the shopping list

'Can I do it? I'm a girl... I dreamt we had a Hoover, a pink one.'

HELEN when Big Brother gives them a carpet sweeper

'Dressed? What, as in clothes?'

HELEN when Big Brother gives them two minutes to get dressed before attending the meteorite crash

'You can't go – nobody else knows how to turn on and off the bloody cooker.'

DEAN to Liz

‘Is there chicken in chick peas?’

HELEN

DIRTY TALK

'It's the only way to stop your hair getting messed up.'

HELEN on making love on top

'Get your tits out every day.'

BRIAN's advice to Narinder when she is up for eviction

'It is shockingly a helluva lot bigger.'

PAUL on the size of his penis when it gets erect

'I've never seen a white one before.'

NARINDER after spotting Brian's willy

'I'll bring nudity, naughtiness and nocturnal activity.'

JOSH's empty promise

'I had really wild dreams, I was locked up with this wild man who wanted to keep girls for sex slaves.'

LIZ

'I just wanted to say Whoaaaaaa!'

NARINDER thanking Big Brother for Josh – before she finds out he's gay

'All my dreams have come to nothing.'

NARINDER when she finds out Josh is gay

'I don't want to be a fuck slave!
I want to be a fuck master.'

LIZ on her birthday

'Thank you for letting me grab your bollocks loads.'

PENNY to Paul, just before she leaves the house

'Sex is just a deep and heightened form of communication with someone.'

LIZ during her dinner date with Dean

'What do you do with the stuff?'

HELEN asks Paul and Brian when they talk about masturbating

'Tissues, of course,'

replies BRIAN

'Pretend to be asleep. Make a cave in your bed. Have a towel there to catch it and go for it.'

LIZ instructs Brian on how to have a 'tommy tank' in the house

'I give up as soon as I'm under the duvet and I hear the camera move. It ruins the mood.'

DEAN on masturbating in the house

'Think of someone on their knees.'

HELEN telling Paul that the jaw ache she has from the cream cracker task is similar to giving oral sex

'Leave it out, H. I'm actually getting wood now.'

PAUL telling Helen to stop talking about it

'I love sex.'

The words PAUL daubs on Helen's back during the portrait painting

'You cannot judge anyone on the size of their knob.'

PAUL

'It was like a wrinkled little shrimp.'

HELEN on seeing Brian's willy when he came out of a cold shower

'Did you touch his tackle?'

BRIAN quizzes Helen on how far she went with Paul

'I've always found people with stuff, but no Elvis.'

BRIAN to DEAN, who replies

'So Elvis didn't even come into the building?'

'Shag, please, get it over with.'

BRIAN about Paul and Helen

'So, will you give me a blow job?'

JOSH jokingly asks Brian, over their 'romantic' dinner

'The best person to dance to is someone I really, really hate. I want to see that rise in your pants. I want to make you sweat. I want to cause you pain. If you upset me, then I will give you hell. I'm a bitch. I'm a hard woman. I don't suffer fools gladly.'

AMMA on lap-dancing

DIRTY TALK

'The game is, women say you can or can't have it, men just want it.'

BUBBLE sums up the battle of the sexes

'The guys out there say that if you can't do the hula hoop it means you are crap in bed, so I'm crap in bed.'

BRIAN during the playground task

'Does it feel like putting it in a pot of warm jelly?'

LIZ asks what sex feels like for a man

‘I love blinking, I do.’

HELEN

FLIRTING

'My little lovely, my one and only, my little love.'

PENNY to Paul

'Blowing farts on my neck is not romantic, it's not going to make me horny.'

PAUL to Penny

'I'm glad I'm big and old because you can get away with stuff.'

PENNY after Paul described her as a 'big old girl'

'If you had a posh accent, you'd be very attractive.'

PENNY to Paul

'That is absolutely amazing.
If only men had nails like that.'

BRIAN to Elizabeth, after she scratches his back with her false nails

'You are really very cuddly.'

PAUL to Helen

'We joked, we flirted, you got hot and bothered, couldn't cope – you so wanted me.'

BUBBLE to Amma

'I am so taking the wrong date tonight.'

BRIAN when Dean dresses up in Brian's clothes as a forfeit for not being nominated

'What's your name? Are you single? Are you seeing anyone? Are you seeing Big Sister?'

A drunken BRIAN chats up Big Brother in the Diary Room

'I said you have nice eyes, and I meant it. I think you are a really nice, sweet guy.'

BRIAN to Josh at their dinner date

'I feel privileged to be one of the luckiest men in Britain.'

PAUL after taking drinks and a cigarette to Amma, Helen and Liz, while the girls are in the jacuzzi together

PAUL, HELEN AND STUFF

'We could sleep in here.'

HELEN to Paul, in the den

'This is all getting out of hand.
Down boy!'

PAUL in the den with Helen

'This is a nightmare, it's not cool.'

PAUL after three hours of extreme frustration in the den with Helen

'Do you run on batteries?'

PAUL to Helen

'It takes two to tango,
and we're both tangoing.'

PAUL to Helen

'I find you almost have to be careful,
especially with the opposite sex.'

LIZ counsels Helen about her relationship with Paul

'I know that when I leave, he ain't
gonna like me at all.'

PAUL on Big G

'It's 60% her, 40% me.'

PAUL to Liz

'I think it was 50–50.'

A dejected HELEN, when Liz tells her what Paul said

'It is potentially *West Side Story* – two groups of family and mates who don't know each other.'

PAUL on his and Helen's families meeting in the studio on eviction night

'Do you think about stuff? Stuff you are gonna do when you get out of here?'
HELEN to Paul

'Yeah, you do think about stuff. In here you want stuff so much and it's cool that you can't have it, but when you get it, it's, like, cool stuff...'
PAUL replies

'You want stuff quite bad but stuff ain't gonna happen in here, is it? But when you actually get stuff it could be breathtaking stuff.'
HELEN to Paul

'Paul talks shit and I talk shit and I like talking shit.'

HELEN

'I love you.'

PAUL to Helen

'I do fancy Helen, I fancy her personality completely.'

PAUL

'You liked it and I liked it and that's the deal.'

PAUL to Helen, about cuddling

'You may get married – you are so, so alike.
Or you could just be really good friends.'

LIZ

'We could still fit in stuff.'

HELEN when Paul tells her they may be too busy to see each other outside

'What for?'

HELEN when Paul asks for her phone number

'I look in your eyes and
all this stuff whizzes past me.'

HELEN describes her feelings for Paul

'It's not the same without Paul.
It takes two to tango in that hut,
with one it's just not the same.'

HELEN revisits the den

'It feels like you forgot your girlfriend's birthday.'

BUBBLE on missing the England match

THE CHICKENS

'That would make it a lot easier to kill them.'

DEAN jokes, after Brian suggests naming the chickens after the Spice Girls

'The embryos of Satan are developing as we speak.'

BRIAN's description of the eggs

'Can you eat cock? Or is it turkey?'

HELEN astonishes the others with her inquiry if the cockerel can be eaten

'They're like dinosaurs.'

BRIAN on the chickens

'We've killed a chicken!'

HELEN after the sickly chicken Princess Leia dies

PADDY THE DOG

'It's living, it's real. It's intelligent.'

LIZ to Amma

'And its name isn't Brian, Dean, Josh, Helen or Amma.'

AMMA says, to which LIZ replies

'Even better, it can't speak.'

'He's evil, Satan.'

BRIAN

'A pathetic excuse for a dog.'

DEAN

'He's the kind of dog you see in Paris in people's handbags.'

HELEN to Brian, who replies

'That's because they're taking them to be put down.'

'I can see your Willy Wonka and I'm not happy about that.'

HELEN to Paddy

'He's gorgeous. I love him.
He's like a little snowball.'

HELEN

'I've seen better-looking dogs.'

BRIAN to Helen, who replies

'Someone could say that about you.'

'I know your perm went
wrong, but don't be upset.'

HELEN to the curly-haired little mutt

'That dog did not warm to anyone here. He did not show any respect. He was given everything for four days. We asked him to do four fucking things, all he does is three.'

BRIAN

'He looks like a gay dog.'

BRIAN

'He's lush.'

HELEN

'He's a snobby dog, he does his own thing.'

BRIAN

'He would have made me breakfast.'

BRIAN on how well he would have trained Paddy if the cameras hadn't been there

'He judged people. He was very materialistic. He reminded me of someone I know – me.'

BRIAN

CONFESSIONS

'I was one of the few Asian or coloured people in my school and it was "Paki this" and "Paki that"... I really fancied one boy and he said he wouldn't go out with me because I was a Paki, and he'd be labelled a Paki lover. Another guy said "You would be quite pretty if you were white."'

NARINDER on her school days in Newcastle

'I've found a new confidence. I still struggle with my body image, with trying to build a new relationship, but I've got myself sussed.'

PENNY on body image

'I always feel weird picking one of those up.'

STUART on his phobia about bras

'I've been an absolute bastard to Josh.'

BRIAN in the Diary Room after his row with Josh

'I've let my little girl down. I only came in to win the money for her, all for her.'

BUBBLE after learning that he is being evicted

ON LIFE IN THE HOUSE

'It's like a prison. I'm locked up in a luxurious prison and I have to do ridiculous things.'
BUBBLE

'Is there anybody there? It looks like TV but it's not. They make us smile for bread and water. My name's not even Brian. I'm just an actor.'
BRIAN calling over the garden fence to the outside world

'I think I'm the only Welsh person in here.'
HELEN

'We don't have to like each other. We're not the Waltons.'

NARINDER

'You're talented, sensational and clever.
You should be so proud you even got here.
You are not gone yet – you could be nominated every week and the public could fucking love you, that mad woman in the kitchen.'

BUBBLE to Penny after her nomination

'I'd be too dangerous with all that money.'

HELEN on the prospect of winning

'If you could walk in and out,
this place would be fantastic.'

LIZ on the 'Big Brother' house

'I could have nominated about six people.'

NARINDER

'I'm emotionally attached to the chickens, to the way we make our food, it's our little way because nobody else is going through it.'

PENNY

'If I feel comfortable wearing a hat in bed in a house I don't know, and that makes me feel at ease, then I don't care what you or anyone else thinks.'

BUBBLE to Brian

'I think of a bus queue with the people
I get on with at the front, and the
people I get on with less well at the back.'

DEAN on his nominations system

'Those infrared cameras can
see under your duvets.'

HELEN

'People say you're a winner to get here,
to get this far. But when your name comes up,
you can't help but feel gutted...'

BUBBLE after being nominated for eviction

'There's less people in the house than we started with.'

HELEN

'It's been a journey of discovery.'

DEAN in the Diary Room

'I wonder which celebrity guys are watching and saying "I love Narinder?"'

NARINDER, to which BRIAN quips

'Stevie Wonder.'

'One thing you realize in here – and this will sound really arty farty – is that you can't stop time. A while back it was Sunday and now it's Wednesday. Tomorrow comes after today, yesterday was behind... In here you really notice how you can't hold on to it, you can't hold on to the moments.'

LIZ being profound

'If you get involved in a confrontation in here it's like World War Three.'

BUBBLE in the Diary Room

'I don't think any cameras are on me right now.'

HELEN to PAUL, who replies

'Yeah, except for the one right in front of us.'

'It's an emotional decision... My heart was telling me it was time to do it as opposed to what my head was telling me.'

DEAN on not nominating Paul

'He looks like Satan on a mission.'

BRIAN catches a glimpse of a cameraman behind one of the mirrors

'It's my destiny

'We had to go through audition after audition and they just jumped over the wall.'
HELEN on the youths who broke into the 'Big Brother' compound

'I'm going to leave this house a cheese-eating, wine-drinking, dog-loving, Tai Chi-doing, book-reading, loving-everyone, backgammon-playing poof!'
BRIAN at the cheese-and-wine party

just pure evil.'

BRIAN after realizing there will be an eviction on Friday the thirteenth

'If there was one perfect person [for the *Big Brother* house] they might be sickening and everyone would want to flatten them. They might be called over-efficient.'

LIZ smarting after Dean and Brian jokingly described her as over-efficient

'Don't drink any more and make sure you switch the cooker off.'

DEAN's advice to Brian and Helen when he leaves them in the house

'We're like two babies and the babysitter has gone.'

HELEN when she and Brian are the final two in the house.

‘You are my fashion guru.’

BRIAN to Bubble

'Can I have a foursome?
I wouldn't sleep with Penny,
and I'd go with the rest of them.'

STUART on which of the girls he would sleep with

'Would you like to repeat your
"Fuck you, arsehole" comment, Penny?
Defend it, explain it or take it back.
I am completely offended. You have
shown yourself out to be quite shallow.'

STUART to Penny

'It was like a railway station with the noise. Then she's in the bed and was scraping her hair like a horse.'

PENNY on her row with Amma

'I could smack her one. I could drag her out of this house by the hair!'

HELEN on Narinder, after the Crappy Cuts row

'She's mincemeat if she comes near me.'

NARINDER on Helen, after the Crappy Cuts row

'I had been here for two weeks and I got respect from four straight guys, I had bonded with the guys, I was settling in. When you walked in I felt this high.'

BRIAN kicking off at Josh in the hot tub

'It's not your turn to speak. You are not in this conversation... Stop shouting at me. I do not tolerate people shouting at me.'

STUART to Amma in the hot tub

'You are a smug, insecure person who feels they need to be better than everyone else around them.'

AMMA to Stuart in the hot tub

'I hope the whole fucking country votes him out on Friday.'

AMMA after her row with Stuart

'My personality, someone like you, I would tear you to pieces... I would shred you to bits... I've allowed you to do everything you've done in here. I've allowed you. In here I am the person in control of this house.'

PAUL to Amma when he accuses her of talking down to him

'I'm not going to allow myself to be matched with a guy in this house who happens to be gay, for the amusement of half of England.'

BRIAN to Josh, in their head-to-head in the boys' room

‘Nobody wants to talk to a girl who can’t pogo.’

HELEN after she fails the playground task

MISSING HOME

'My dog, friends and sex.'

JOSH on what he misses

'Open fields, open space, going for walks, talking to people I know. Freedom of speech and freedom of movement. Fresh asparagus.'

LIZ on what she misses

'Chocolate, crisps and shopping.'

BRIAN on what he misses

'Light switches, floor mats and hot water.'

LIZ

'I'd like more food, more chocolate, more alcohol and being able to go out. That would be easier on everybody. Go to work, come back in, go back out, go out and teach dancing, come back in and have a hot tub. But that's just Helen living in Helen's little world.'

HELEN

'I'd love to do a day's work, anything.'

DEAN

SLEEPTALK

'Be prepared.
Be really, really prepared.'

PAUL

'What the fuck's wrong with it?
Where the fuck is it? It's nice to see you.
You didn't have to come all the way up.'

DEAN

'Thank you for picking me,
everybody that did. That's cool.'

PAUL

‘Stroke my hair, I’m gonna be famous.’

JOSH

'I am top

'But what can be weird is that people
just don't get that I...'

PAUL

'Do not drink alcohol... Don't talk about
all the popular dogs in the world.'

DEAN

'It's so unnecessary. Amma, I can understand.'

PAUL

secret.' ▪ PAUL

'Concentrate.'

LIZ

'Let me put my point across... Everyone can say whatever they want. Is that cool? Just so everyone gets a fair crack of the whip.'

PAUL

'I hate you lot.'

DEAN

‘BIG BROTHER WILL GET BACK TO YOU.’